P9-CFB-372

DISCARD

SHORTY
&
CLEM
BLAST OFF!

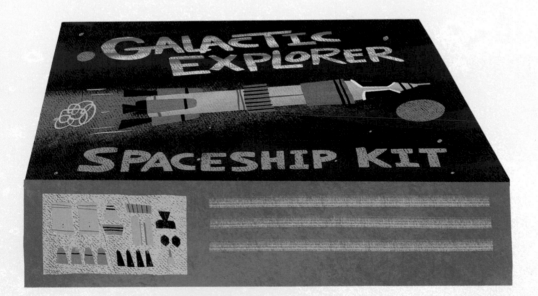

Michael Slack

HARPER
An Imprint of HarperCollinsPublishers

Shorty & Clem Blast Off!
Copyright © 2018 by Michael Slack
All rights reserved. Manufactured in China.
No part of this book may be used or reproduced in any manner
whatsoever without written permission except in the case of brief
quotations embodied in critical articles and reviews. For information
address HarperCollins Children's Books, a division of HarperCollins
Publishers, 195 Broadway, New York, NY 10007.
www.harpercollinschildrens.com

ISBN 978-0-06-242159-3

The artist used Photoshop to create the digital
illustrations for this book.
18 19 20 21 22   SCP   10 9 8 7 6 5 4 3 2 1
❖
First Edition

To Jackson DeMarco Borg

That's OK, Shorty. I've got this.
Are you sure you don't need my help?

Shorty, I can do it myself.
Come on, Clem. Please! Please! Please! Please!

Hey!

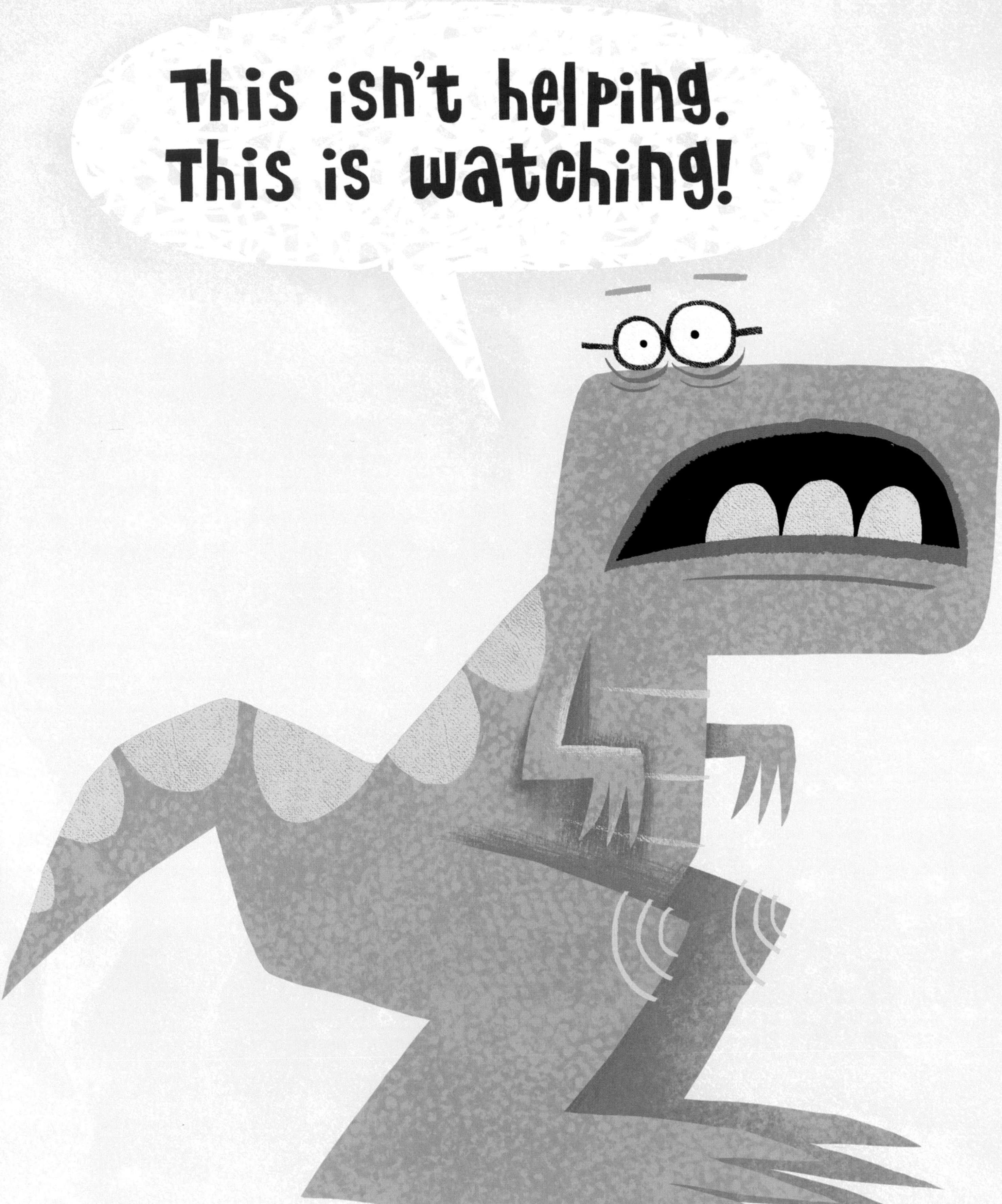
This isn't helping.
This is watching!

-sigh-

And a handy bendy tail.